IMAGES
of America

RANTOUL AND
CHANUTE AIR FORCE BASE

MOSAIC
OF
CHANUTE FIELD & RANTOUL ILL.

PHOTOGRAPHED & ASSEMBLED BY
CHANUTE FIELD PHOTOGRAPHIC SECTION
OCT. 19, 1940

In 1922, the Air Service Photographic School transferred from Langley Field, Virginia, to Chanute Field, Illinois. One of the results of this move is a rich heritage of aerial photography of the Rantoul area. Here a photo mosaic produced by the Chanute Field Photographic Section shows Rantoul and Chanute Field as of October 19, 1940. (Chanute Air Museum.)

ON THE COVER: The self-proclaimed "world's first regular airplane express service" made a delivery to Rantoul on September 3, 1919. A checker-winged Society Brand Clothes Curtiss JN-4D Jenny biplane out of Chicago landed at Chanute Field with a clothes shipment destined for Bohlen's Clothing Shop of Rantoul (see pages 58–59). (Rantoul Historical Society.)

IMAGES
of America

RANTOUL AND
CHANUTE AIR FORCE BASE

Mark D. Hanson

ARCADIA
PUBLISHING

Published by Arcadia Publishing
Charleston, South Carolina

Printed in the United States of America

Library of Congress Control Number: 2011920703

For all general information, please contact Arcadia Publishing:
Telephone 843-853-2070
Fax 843-853-0044
E-mail sales@arcadiapublishing.com
For customer service and orders:
Toll-Free 1-888-313-2665

Visit us on the Internet at www.arcadiapublishing.com

*To the people of Rantoul and Chanute Air Force
Base, hopefully this book opens a window into your
history through which you will want to look.*

CONTENTS

ACKNOWLEDGMENTS

This project is about imagery introducing the story of Rantoul and Chanute Air Force Base (AFB). The images are the real authors. Thus this book would not be possible without the rich photographic and visual collections held by the Rantoul Historical Society and Chanute Air Museum. Founded in 1973 and 1992, respectively, these institutions diligently collect, preserve, and interpret the rich history and legacy of the village of Rantoul and Chanute Air Force Base. Their tireless efforts are often unseen and underappreciated. A debt of gratitude is owed to the staff, volunteers, and members of both institutions for their valiant endeavors to save and protect our historical inheritance.

Very special thanks are extended to Jim Cheek and Kaye Heath from the Rantoul Historical Society for offering crucial knowledge, insight, and support and providing unrestricted access to the Rantoul Historical Society's collections. Their formidable combined knowledge about the history of Rantoul and its people were an indispensable asset.

I would also like to thank the Octave Chanute Aerospace Heritage Foundation Board of Directors and Chanute Air Museum collections and exhibits committee for allowing me to pursue this project and utilize my position as their curator to facilitate the use of the museum's photography collections; and thanks to fellow "museum marine," Robyn York.

This book was breathed to life with an inquiry by Arcadia Publishing acquisitions editor Jeff Ruetsche, hammered into shape by insights, comments, and critiques from Ron Eagan and Gussie Desigio, and strengthened by research assistance from Jim Eldridge at the Chanute Air Museum, Marnie Hess at the Champaign County Historical Archives, Thomas Berry, archivist for the Historical Construction Equipment Association, and David Parfitt with www.steel-wheels.net.

Most importantly, the grace, mercy, love, and support shown by my beautiful wife and amazing children ultimately allowed me and drove me to complete this project. I pray you will be proud of the end product and believe it was worth the price.

INTRODUCTION

The rich history and legacy of the village of Rantoul is often overshadowed by the equally rich legacy of the former Chanute Air Force Base. The histories of both are inseparably intertwined, each contributing to define the nature and character of the other, and in fact part of the same story. Thus any attempt to document the history and legacy of one requires the inclusion of the other. No single volume can tell the whole story, so this work is meant as a visual primer.

The village of Rantoul was founded near a stand of trees on the gently rolling east-central Illinois prairie known as Mink Grove, or Nieps-wah, a Native American term for "mink" or "abounding in mink." The area was characterized by wild walnut trees, open water, and an abundance of game and served as a seasonal hunting and gathering grounds dating back to 6500 B.C. for Native American peoples and their precursors.

Archa Campbell and his wife, Eliza, became Mink Grove's first settlers. Campbell filed for 40 acres of public land in 1849 and settled in 1850. He primarily raised stock and the forage to feed them but also endured attacks upon his livelihood by "oppressively abundant" wildlife. J. S. Lothrop recounts Campbell finally driving off a herd of marauding wild hogs from his cornfield, but only after killing four and wounding one.

Settlers came and went, but Guy B. Chandler, John Penfield, and Guy D. Penfield were the area's next pioneers with long-term intentions. Mink Grove's settlement was leisurely, but the railroad initiated a period of development, investment, and growth.

On September 20, 1850, the U.S. Congress approved an act granting federal lands to the states of Illinois, Mississippi, and Alabama to accommodate a railroad stretching from Chicago, Illinois, in the north to Mobile, Alabama, in the south. A group of eastern investors formed the Illinois Central Railroad Company, which sought these federal railroad lands in Illinois for development. Noted financiers of the company included the British horticulturist and architect Joseph Paxton and future British chancellor of the exchequer and prime minister William Gladstone. Robert Rantoul Jr., an Illinois Central Railroad director, was sent to Springfield, Illinois, in 1851 as the new company's representative and promoter to make a case before the Illinois State Legislature.

Robert Rantoul Jr. was a Massachusetts lawyer and politician. An idealist, Rantoul was opposed to slavery, for labor unions, and a strong supporter of expanding railroads in the west. He saw the economic benefit of railroad expansion but also deeper geopolitical potential. Rantoul stated, "A railroad . . . running from Chicago to Mobile will do more to connect the Union in enduring bands than all the windy declamations of all the demagogues that have spouted in legislative halls." Robert Rantoul Jr. died in 1852 at the age of 47.

The Illinois Legislature, via a bill signed by Gov. Augustus C. French and apparently opposed by Abraham Lincoln, incorporated the Central Illinois Railroad Company in February 1851 and granted it land designated by the federal act of 1850. The first land grant railroad in the United States was born. The company was chartered to build a railroad from the southern terminus of the Illinois and Michigan Canal south to Cairo, Illinois, with branch lines extending to Chicago and through Galena, Illinois, to Dunleith, Illinois, on the Mississippi River opposite Dubuque, Iowa. Preliminary surveys began the following spring.

Built by hand and horse team, the Central Illinois Railroad was completed from Chicago to Urbana, Illinois, on July 24, 1854. For Mink Grove and the surrounding area, the coming of the railroad was a life-changing spectacle to behold. The railroad opened trade and commerce opportunities and provided a vital artery for emigration that drove a rapid expansion of agricultural activities. Marshlands and swamp areas were drained and the rich ground turned into farmland.

By 1855, the Illinois Central Railroad station at Gaynor's Crossing was named after Robert Rantoul by the railroad's president, William P. Burrall. However, Guy P. Chandler suggested the Rantoul station be relocated to Mink Grove. Chandler, who had acquired large tracts of land in the area, offered to donate several lots to the railroad to facilitate the move. The offer was accepted, and the station was moved three miles north in 1856. The town that grew up around the station became known as Rantoul.

The village of Rantoul was platted by Guy D. Penfield in 1856 and continued to grow as an agricultural community fed by a railroad economy. Thanks to the industry and vigor of its early citizenry, J. S. Lothrop wrote of Rantoul, "A more flourishing, comely, wide-awake and inviting village cannot be found in all the Northwest."

Rantoul's growth was not without disaster. Fire had been a constant concern as early as 1860, and a blaze in 1899 destroyed the southern half of Rantoul's business district. But the ferocity and destruction of the fire of 1901 was never before seen. On August 9, 1901, an Illinois Central southbound train, running late, roared through Rantoul shortly after 11:00 a.m. Sparks or hot cinders from the passing locomotive ignited the Goff and Yates grain elevator. Fueled by strong winds from the southwest, high temperatures, and drought conditions, the conflagration soon raged out of control despite the rapid response of the Rantoul fire department and assistance from firefighters and equipment from both Paxton and Champaign. The fire raged down Sangamon Avenue, nearly destroying the entire business district. John Gray, whose family lost their harness shop that day, remembered the fire "sort of skipped," first burning down the Baptist church and damaging the new Catholic church still under construction on the corner of Grove Street and Route 45 (Century Boulevard). The blaze finally wore itself out on the outskirts of town. In the end, 54 businesses and nine homes were destroyed at an estimated loss of $314,000. Almost immediately business owners set up temporary shops, and the task of rebuilding got underway.

World War I erupted in 1914, and despite an original policy of isolationism and proclamations of neutrality, the United States declared war on Germany on April 6, 1917. Preparatory efforts were made for the nation's defense prior to the declaration of war, but military aviation was entirely inadequate. The Aviation Section of the U.S. Army Signal Corps consisted of only one aero squadron comprised of 250 aircraft. Congress quickly appropriated $640 million to meet the severe military aviation shortfall, including the construction of new flying fields.

Champaign County, Illinois, was chosen for the site of a temporary army flying field, and a committee was established by the University of Illinois to select an appropriate site. William H. Wheat immediately offered the village of Rantoul as a suitable location. Wheat, president of Rantoul's First National Bank, showed inspectors three different sites. The one best suited consisted of 640 acres of farmland south east of Rantoul owned by L. H. Alpers, M. Christie, J. G. Flessner, J. M. McCullough, and the Steffler and West Company. The owners, however, refused to lease their land to government, so Wheat immediately formed a land syndicate that bought all 640 acres for $208,000.

After heated debate, the Rantoul site was chosen over a competing site in Bondville, west of the city of Champaign, on May 21, 1917. The Rantoul site was chosen because it was level with few obstructions. It was close to the railroad, and the village of Rantoul could supply water and electrical service. The new facility was named Chanute Field in honor of Illinois aviation pioneer, confidant and friend of the Wright brothers, and accomplished civil engineer Octave Chanute.

The contract to build Chanute Field was given to English Brothers Construction of Champaign on May 22, 1917, with the expectation that construction would be complete in 60 days. Building materials began arriving on site on May 25, and work began in earnest on June 4. At the peak of construction, 2,000 men, 200 teams of horses, three steam shovels, and multiple steam tractors were working on Chanute Field, with a payroll reaching $96,000 per week.

The construction of Chanute Field was an economic boom for Rantoul; money and people flowed into the village at a rapid rate, with both workers and visitors coming to see the construction spectacle. Townspeople rented out rooms, the Tremont Hotel added on, and a new housing development sprang up. The atmosphere was compared to a celebration, but with the boom also came increased crime, a shortage of food and retail goods, traffic congestion, and a housing shortage.

Chanute's first commander, Capt. Charles C. Benedict, arrived in late June, and on July 4 the first airplane arrived. Maj. James L. Dunsworth arrived shortly thereafter and took command. He ordered flight training to begin on July 17, with Curtiss Jenny biplanes taking to the air on July 18 from "dawn to dusk." Chanute Field was completed on July 22, 1917, at a cost of about $1 million and was officially accepted on July 31. On August 20, Chanute Field was closed to visitors. Dunsworth stated, "We haven't time to entertain visitors. Our business is to turn out skilled air pilots for the European battle lines."

As World War I drew to a close in November 1918, Chanute Field had trained countless pilots, of which 1st Lt. Charles R. D'Olive, Maj. Reid M. Chambers, and Capt. Reed G. Landis became fighter aces. Chanute also either hosted or recruited 12 aero squadrons that fought over Europe. Nevertheless, on November 19, flight training was stopped. In December, the remaining aero squadrons were demobilized and the airplanes shipped out. Chanute Field, previously staffed with well over 1,000 men, was drawn down to less than 400. The installation became a storage depot for OX-5 aircraft engines and paint. In August 1919, the recommendation was made in Washington, D.C., that Chanute should be closed.

Appropriations were passed on February 11, 1920, with which Chanute Field was finally purchased by the U.S. government, but Chanute's decline continued unabated, and the facilities fell into disrepair. Then on January 4, 1921, the Air Service Mechanics School was transferred to Chanute Field, followed by the entire Air Corps Training School. Chanute's long and storied service as a premier technical training facility had begun. Beginning in 1936, Chanute Field's great renaissance began. Despite over a decade of heated debate swirling around persistent rumors and recommendations for closure, Chanute Field was finally saved as a permanent military installation, and massive appropriations bills were passed to rebuild the field into a state-of-the-art technical training facility.

By mid-1941, on the brink of World War II, massive construction projects were coming to an end—including four large aircraft hangars, a network of concrete runways, barracks, theaters, a hospital, headquarters building, and family housing. Following the attack on Pearl Harbor, Chanute Field quickly mobilized to support the war effort. The technical training mission remained, but a massive influx of new recruits and volunteers led to a critical housing shortage. Also on March 22, 1941, the first all-black fighter squadron was activated at Chanute Field. Formed without pilots, for the purpose of training the officer corps and ground support personnel, the 99th Pursuit Squadron was the first unit of what later became popularly known as the Tuskegee Airmen. The Women's Army Air Corps School was established in early 1944. After World War II, Chanute Field became a primary separation center, mustering out 100 men per day.

Along with Chanute, Rantoul mobilized during World War II as well. Families opened their doors to airmen away from home on holidays and aggressively participated in war bond and defense stamp drives. Rationing began in 1942. To help provide recreational opportunities, local organizations such as St. Malachy Church and the Masonic lodge opened servicemen's centers. Most importantly, Rantoul contributed and sacrificed sons, brothers, and fathers to all branches of U.S. military services.

Following World War II, Rantoul lost Chanute Field but, with the formation of the U.S. Air Force in 1948, gained Chanute Air Force Base. At this time, Chanute was also undergoing a major technological shift with the introduction and adoption of jet engines and the required technical training curricula to support them. Chanute also found itself building up for the Korean War in

1951. Again a housing shortage seemed imminent, and both Rantoul and the base saw a marked increase in the number of homes constructed. After the armistice ended armed conflict in Korea, events focused attention on the developing Cold War and the military and political campaign to neutralize and deter the Soviet Union. Nuclear deterrence became a national defense strategy, and Chanute again embraced technological advancements and the new technical training they required. The Vietnam War soon followed. Boeing B-52 bombers and intercontinental missiles became training mainstays, along with fire, weather, and jet engine training.

As Chanute Air Force Base continued to adapt, grow, and contribute to the larger mission of the U.S. Air Force, Rantoul continued to adapt and grow and contribute along with it. The relationship between Rantoul and Chanute was symbiotic. In 1955, spurred by requirements at the base, Rantoul received its first dial phone system and was classed as an "impacted area" due to Chanute and the large number of service people it drew. Rantoul went from one grade school to six virtually overnight, and federal funding was available for major infrastructure upgrades, such as a new wastewater treatment plant and road improvements.

Unfortunately the relationship between Rantoul and Chanute was not to last. Chanute Air Force Base found itself on Defense Base Closure and Realignment Commission closure lists in the 1980s. After the base dodged one listing, a second could not be avoided. Chanute Air Force Base officially closed on September 30, 1993. The socioeconomic impacts on Rantoul were devastating, and over a decade later the effects are still being felt. Today a new chapter in Rantoul's history is being written, and it proves to be as engaging and significant as those already complete.

One

A FLOURISHING AND INVITING VILLAGE

Robert Rantoul Jr. was the Massachusetts lawyer and politician responsible for acquiring the Illinois Central Railroad charter from the Illinois State Legislature. He never lived in Illinois and died before the railroad was completed. Rantoul posthumously became the town's namesake in 1855. A city in Kansas is also named Rantoul. (Rantoul Historical Society.)

Early Rantoul farmers were proud of their families, their livestock, and their farms. For many, agriculture proved quite profitable. Likely taken in the late 1890s, this photograph documents the Chumbley farm. From left to right are farmhand Clarence Brown, Roy Chumbley (age 12), Frank Chumbley, Marion Chumbley (age 10), and Delia Chumbley. Delia is holding Nell, the family's "gentle driving horse." (Rantoul Historical Society.)

Farming in Rantoul was and continues to be a family affair. In this unidentified 1910s family photograph during the threshing season near Rantoul, multiple generations pose with the fruits of their labor and the tools of their trade. On the far right, a steam-powered tractor, likely built by the Advance Thresher Company of Battle Creek, Michigan, powers the threshing machine in the center. On the far left are the horse-drawn wagons that remained vital agricultural tools until the large-scale adoption of internal combustion engine tractors. (Rantoul Historical Society.)

Charles Heffernan's horses and plow turn over an old cornfield west of Rantoul in the late 1800s or early 1900s. From the arrival of the first settlers in 1848 through the present day, agriculture remains an important economic force in Rantoul. Before the advent of the farm tractor in the early 1910s, teams of horses provided farm power, creating a demand for secondary businesses such as harness and blacksmith shops. Though the plow looks relatively small, five horses are needed to pull it. (Rantoul Historical Society.)

In this 1890s photograph of Gray's Harness Shop in Rantoul are, from left to right, John Gray, Will Gray, and a Mr. Green. With horses a primary mode of transportation as well as being used for farm power, businesses sprang up in Rantoul to provide the necessary goods and services for an equestrian society. Gray's Harness Shop was one such enterprise. Unfortunately the shop pictured here was destroyed by the great 1901 fire. (Rantoul Historical Society.)

Benjamin J. Gifford envisioned a competitive railroad from West Lebanon, Indiana, through Rantoul to Le Roy, Illinois. In 1873, a charter was granted to the Havana, Rantoul, and Eastern Railroad—later the Rantoul Railroad Company but best known as the Shortline. Construction was completed in 1879. Unfortunately the venture was unsuccessful, and the Illinois Central would take control of the line in 1887. Here an Illinois Central Shortline locomotive sits at the water tower at the rail yard and roundhouse north of Rantoul sometime between 1880 and 1910. (Rantoul Historical Society.)

An agricultural community fueled by the business of the railroad, Rantoul's economy and commerce boomed. Many family-owned enterprises would continue for generations. Williams Hardware Store opened in 1862 at 107 East Sangamon Avenue. Taken sometime in the late 1890s, this photograph shows, from left to right, proprietor O. E. Williams, Fred Musson, and William Hulls. A variety of goods includes familiar brand names such as Lufkin, Sterno, and DeLaval. (Rantoul Historical Society.)

During the late 1890s, "safety" bicycles, with pneumatic, equally sized tires and rear-wheel chain drive became all the rage for both men and women. Rantoul was no exception, especially since Chicago was a center for bicycle manufacturers. Here C. C. Condit holds up a bicycle for the camera. Ed Beal looks on at left. The back row of onlookers includes, from left to right, Al Lovejoy, John Gray, Charlie Gray, Ed Hamilton, and Willard Gray. The bicycle sports a "Sweetheart" sprocket. (Rantoul Historical Society.)

As they are today, sports have been a significant part of Rantoul's citizens' recreation and free time. School sports are especially important and have been from very early on. Pictured here is the Rantoul High School football team in 1896. Today Rantoul still cheers for the local school teams and those from the University of Illinois. (Rantoul Historical Society.)

15

This undated photograph of Campbell Avenue east of the railroad tracks projects, in the words of J. S. Lothrop, "thrift, comfort and wealth" with its wide street, large tree-lined boulevards, and ribbons of sidewalk. Campbell Avenue was also known locally as "Railroaders Avenue" due to the large number of railroad workers who lived there. On the right, a man in a bowler hat is mowing his lawn. (Rantoul Historical Society.)

Rantoul established a municipal waterworks in the early 1880s. In 1896, the first electric light plant was built on the northwest corner of North Ohio and West Grove Streets, and the municipal water tower was moved near that site. A new brick water tower, topped by a 64,000-gallon cypress tank, replaced the old tower in 1903. Pictured here are the light plant and 1903 water tower. The arc light atop the water tower was a favorite target of youths armed with slingshots. (Rantoul Historical Society.)

Two

A MODEL TOWN RISEN FROM ASHES AND RUIN

Disaster struck Rantoul in 1901 when a great fire destroyed 54 businesses and nine homes. This image shows the complete devastation, more reminiscent of bombed-out Europe after World War II than a rural town in east central Illinois. The fire was blamed on sparks from a train locomotive. Men and boys work amongst the rubble; they appear to be neatly stacking reusable bricks. (Rantoul Historical Society.)

This photograph documents more of the destruction following Rantoul's fire of 1901. The chimneys and smokestacks stand sentinel over the ruins of an unidentified building, while people sift through the rubble near stacks of salvaged bricks. The only downtown buildings to survive the fire were the blacksmith shop, Martin House, and an implement building. A passenger train like the one credited with starting the blaze sits in the background. (Rantoul Historical Society.)

Looking south across Garrard Street, the ruins on the right are the remains of the Trade Palace building, the Arlington hotel is in the center, and the destroyed Opera House just visible on the far right. Despite the severity of the damage, in the lower foreground is a pristine stretch of herringbone brick sidewalk. (Rantoul Historical Society.)

The citizenry of Rantoul were understandably in shock after experiencing the inferno that destroyed the heart of their town, but within a matter of weeks they rose above the hardship and began rebuilding. By October 1901, barely two months after the fire, no fewer than 35 new brick buildings were under construction. Here a crowd of people surveys the damage, likely just east of the tracks on Sangamon Avenue. Men on the right appear to be addressing downed power lines across the street. (Rantoul Historical Society.)

In 1899, the First National Bank was established by a group of Rantoul citizens. In 1901, it was destroyed by fire along with the Collison Brothers and Company Bank. This image is believed to show the vault from one of these banks. There is a large crest above the door; just visible on the right is what appears to be the vault door handle, and on the left are the heavy door hinges. (Rantoul Historical Society.)

Despite being destroyed by the 1901 fire, the First National Bank quickly rose from the ashes to continue doing business in this temporary shack. After the fire, Collison Brothers and Company Bank and the First National Bank consolidated. Under the leadership of Fred Collison and Herbert West, the First National Bank building that still stands today was built on the northeast corner of Sangamon Avenue and Garrard Street. The new building became one of the grandest structures in the area, costing over $20,000 to complete. (Rantoul Historical Society.)

Before widespread television and radio, newspapers were the heartbeat of communication. In 1901, the homes of both the *Rantoul Press* and *Rantoul News* were destroyed by the fire. This is the newly constructed Rantoul News Building on south Garrard Street. There appears to be a fire hydrant out front. (Rantoul Historical Society.)

Another business destroyed by the fire of 1901 was J. M. Gray and Sons Harness shop, known for its "quality" products and "fair dealings." The Grays rebuilt their shop on the south side of Sangamon Avenue. Shown here is their new building. The second story served as a photography studio. The people standing out front are believed to be members of the Gray family, and the little girl in the white dress is identified as Opal Gray. (Rantoul Historical Society.)

In 1902, possibly in conjunction with Fourth of July festivities, a hot-air balloon ascension was conducted on the streets of Rantoul, foreshadowing the aviation legacy of Chanute Field. The balloon's flight was obviously a family event, with children in the crowd, a man holding a baby on the right, and a woman with a baby carriage on the left near the building. (Rantoul Historical Society.)

The inconvenient mud inherent to dirt roads rapidly became unacceptable to farmers, recreational cyclists, and automobile enthusiasts. Starting with the Federal Aid Road Act of 1916, improving American roadways became a national priority. This photograph, shot in the early 1900s, shows a concrete paver and crew at work in Rantoul. At the front of the machine, also known as a dry batch paver, is a large hopper that lowered for workmen to empty wheelbarrow loads of aggregate and

cement into. The hopper was then raised to dump the material into the circular mixing chamber and facilitate pulling the paver forward. Concrete was discharged out the back via the long chute. Water lines run to the top of the machine, and wooden forms are evident along the edges of the roadway. Note the racial segregation of the workmen. (Rantoul Historical Society.)

Children are the lifeblood and future for a small town, and many of Rantoul's young people chose to stay rather than be lured away to larger cities. Early on, Rantoul made provisions for the education of its youth, a tradition that would continue to be achieved through the years. Here, from left to right around 1905, Hardey Talbot, Marjorie Smith, Jessie Robinson, Lillian Robinson, Opal Gray, and Harold Gray ride a teeter-totter, possibly outside the Rantoul School building. (Rantoul Historical Society.)

Catholic Church. Rantoul, Ill.

From its earliest settlement, Rantoul has been a town of diverse religious beliefs. A Sunday school was established in 1857 to provide "moral instruction" for the town's children. From those humble beginnings sprung forth Baptist, Catholic, Lutheran, Methodist, Presbyterian, and other Christian traditions. Shown here sometime after 1901 is one of Rantoul's most distinguishable landmarks—St. Malachy Catholic Church on the corner of Grove Street and Route 45 (Century Boulevard). (Rantoul Historical Society.)

Taken sometime between 1905 and 1912 by Orum Johnson and looking southeast, this photograph shows a rebuilt downtown Rantoul. In the center are the Illinois Central Railroad depot, stockyard, and loading chutes with a northbound train inbound. The tall building on the left is the Neal Opera House. On the right is the Hayward grain elevator, and just visible equidistant between them is the Rantoul Livery stable. (Rantoul Historical Society.)

Fred Collison was a prominent Rantoul banker and president of the First National Bank following the 1901 fire. In 1903, Collison built a new home at 405 East Belle Street at the princely cost of $6,000 to $7,000. In this idyllic scene of Belle Street, Collison's home is the first on the left. (Rantoul Historical Society.)

Rantoul has been predominantly a civic-minded community. Though hard work was the expected norm, celebration and fellowship also played an important role in village life. The two images shown here record a town barbecue held on September 8, 1909. The photograph above depicts the activity on Garrard Street. The building on the right houses the G. F. Sales Grocery store under the large awning and Steffler and West Dry Goods. This structure is also home to the First National Bank. Below, workmen armed with shovels tend to the barbecue pit as well-dressed citizens look on in the background. (Rantoul Historical Society.)

Even before the coming of Chanute Field, Rantoul was a patriotic community that was proud of its veterans. Here citizens line up in preparation for a Decoration Day parade around 1910. The procession appears to contain schoolchildren on the right and possibly Rantoul veterans on the left, with the American flag and what appear to be lapel badges on their coats. (Rantoul Historical Society.)

Physician and surgeon Dr. Dan Cole worked from his west side home. Pictured here around 1910, Dr. Cole and an unidentified travelling companion sit atop a Brush Runabout automobile, while Cole's wife, Ethel, looks on. The doctor's "shingle" is on a tree to the right. In 1910, a Brush Runabout cost less than $500. (Rantoul Historical Society.)

Not surprisingly, with the prominence of rail travel and commerce in the Rantoul area, accidents were not exceptionally uncommon. In these undated photographs, likely taken around 1910, two Illinois Central Shortline locomotives have collided near Fisher, Illinois. The image above clearly shows the debris and damage to the locomotives caused by the crash. The photograph below offers another view of the wreck. The railroaders standing in the center are identified as Gordie Douglas (left) and Vest Dongahue. Crowds of curious sightseers are in both images. (Rantoul Historical Society.)

This 1910 view looking east down Sangamon Avenue from the Illinois Central tracks is representative of the commercial diversity of Rantoul's business district. The farthest structure on the left is the First National Bank building with a hotel just up the street. On the right, across from the bank and heading west, are Miller's Clothing Store, Grays Harness shop (characterized by the sloping second-story photography studio windows), a meat market, dentist's office, post office, the Rantoul Press Office, August Johnson's shop, H. B. Clark's jewelry store, and Hendrick's Store. (Chanute Air Museum.)

Rantoul's Illinois Central Railroad depot was the location of political whistle-stop speeches. This image shows Illinois governor Charles S. Deneen addressing a crowd from a railcar on February 27, 1912. The assembly appears to be a diverse mix of both businessmen and laborers. Not surprisingly, women are largely absent; this is possibly due to the cold weather but perhaps since they were not able to vote until 1920. (Rantoul Historical Society.)

Shown here is the Ekblaw and Peterson Grocers delivery wagon around 1914; the driver is unidentified. Ekblaw and Peterson's original business was destroyed in the 1901 fire at a loss of $10,000 and with an insurance reimbursement of only $5,000. The wagon features spartan accommodations for the driver and the store's phone number on the side. (Rantoul Historical Society.)

Well into the 1900s, the horse remained a vital mode of transportation and a primary engine for work. Thus horse shows and auctions remained commonplace on the streets of Rantoul. Pictured here is a horse show or auction in front of Gray's Harness shop in 1915. The rider in the center appears to be wearing a sash that may distinguish him as a judge. Also of interest are the large advertisements in the background to the left for the musical comedy *Wizards of Wiseland*. (Rantoul Historical Society.)

Three

OUR BUSINESS IS AIR PILOTS

Chanute Field's namesake was Octave A. Chanute. A naturalized American citizen from France, Chanute was a renowned civil engineer by profession. He also developed a creosote process for preserving wooden railroad ties and telephone poles. When Chanute retired in 1890, he turned his energy to the scientific problem of flight, becoming a clearinghouse for aviation research, an experimenter, and a contemporary of the Wright Brothers. Chanute died in Chicago, Illinois, in 1910. (Chanute Air Museum.)

Chanute Field was originally constructed with a large flying field bordered to the north by a long, narrow organization of hangars, workshops, barracks, and administration buildings. Shown here is a c. 1917 view to the west down one of Chanute's main streets. Ford Model T automobiles are conspicuous as is the windsock to the upper left. (Chanute Air Museum.)

Taken on September 7, 1917, not long after construction was finished, this photograph shows the far eastern end of Chanute Field looking west. The main gravel road simply turns into a rutted dirt track in the foreground, and the power poles still exhibit the mounds of dirt at their bases left behind from their installation. The buildings with screened porches on the right are believed to be officers' quarters. (Chanute Air Museum.)

Chanute Field was built in 1917 as a temporary installation to train pilots for World War I. Flight training began before the field was finished, and planes in the air became a great spectacle. A formation of Curtiss JN-4 Jenny biplanes is shown over a newly completed Chanute Field with Rantoul lying to the northwest. No formal runways are visible; airplanes simply operated from the open field adjacent to the flight-line tracks. (Chanute Air Museum.)

Despite Chanute Field being closed to visitors, curious folks still flocked to the area to see the new phenomenon of flight. Rantoul's economy reaped the benefits. On September 30, 1917, the road west of the flying field was lined with automobiles and spectators intent on enjoying a Sunday afternoon watching airplanes. (Chanute Air Museum.)

Maj. James L. Dunsworth was Chanute Field's first operational commander. Under his leadership, flight training began on July 17, 1917, five days before construction was complete and 14 days before the U.S. Army Air Corps officially accepted the field. Flight operations brought throngs of civilians to the base to see for themselves the spectacle of flight. Dunsworth quickly removed the distraction and inconvenience of crowds of curious sightseers by closing the installation to all visitors without a pass. Chanute did not have time to entertain when its training was needed for the battlefields and skies of Europe during World War I. (Chanute Air Museum.)

Having served with General Pershing in the Mexican Expedition of 1916, Maj. Roy S. Brown commanded the 16th Aero Squadron that flew Chanute's first 23 Curtiss JN-4 biplanes from Chicago to Rantoul on July 9, 1917. The squadron's flight was credited as the largest formation of airplanes to ever complete a cross-county journey. Amid a circus atmosphere, the press recorded, "like huge birds the machines descended gradually to the ground." During the summer of 1917, Major Brown was in command of all flight operations at Chanute Field and command of the 16th Aero Squadron given to Capt. W. W. Spain. (Chanute Air Museum.)

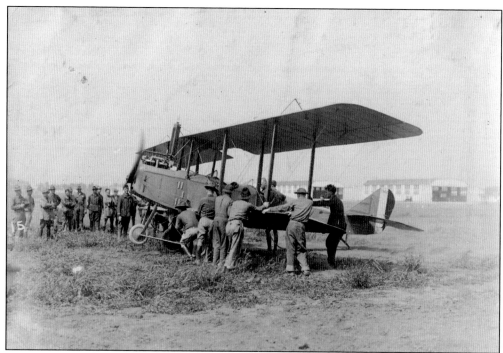

Designed by Charles H. Day, who drew up plans for the Curtiss JN-4, the Standard SJ-1 was a second-rate training aircraft at best. Powered by the rough-running and unreliable Hall-Scott A-7a engine, SJ-1s served at Chanute nonetheless. Pictured here, Major Brown runs up SJ-1, ship number T962, during the summer of 1917 as ground personnel hold the airplane. The vertically protruding radiator and exhaust stack of the Hall-Scott engine and the unique tricycle landing gear configuration help identify the aircraft. (Chanute Air Museum.)

Spectators on the ground would have sought for a glimpse such as this. Here a Mr. Gordon waves goodbye as Lieutenant Schroeder and Major Connelly take to the air in a JN-4 Jenny. Gordon is standing at the end of a gravel flight line extending into the flying field. (Chanute Air Museum.)

For ground crews and maintenance personnel, flight operations were a labor-intensive endeavor. This undated photograph shows the personnel left behind after the successful take-off of a De-Havilland DH-4. The men are wearing dirty coveralls. American-built DH-4s were the only aircraft from the United States to see combat in World War I and were developed into some 60 different variants. (Chanute Air Museum.)

Flight operations from an aircrew perspective were drastically different than those of a civilian spectator or military ground crewman. Lieutenant Dodge and Private Lyons are viewed in their JN-4 Jenny from an altitude of 3,000 feet above the farm fields around Rantoul. The photograph was taken from a sister ship in their formation, the lower wing of which frames the image on the left. (Chanute Air Museum.)

Taken from the rear cockpit of a Standard SJ-1, this photograph shows the horizon over a Rantoul area farm in 1917. Wing supports bracket the left of the image, but more noticeable are the large vertical engine radiator and exhaust stack virtually eliminating forward visibility. (Chanute Air Museum.)

Flight training operations in 1917 and 1918 have been described as lasting from "dawn until dusk" on a daily basis. Consequently airplane accidents were not uncommon, and local farm fields and country roads became emergency landing zones and crash sites. Pictured in a grain field, around 1917 or 1918, is Chanute Field JN-4 no. 130. With the plane suffering engine trouble, the pilot was forced to make an emergency landing. (Chanute Air Museum.)

The aircraft of the early 1900s were incredibly frail, temperamental, and dangerous in comparison to their contemporary counterparts. Most were made primarily of wood with doped fabric covering, and the only substantial metal component was the engine. On the morning of September 18, 1917, Sgt. H. M. Rice spiraled at low altitude and catastrophically crashed JN-4 no. 9 into a cornfield. Broken wood and wrinkled fabric are clearly evident. (Chanute Air Museum.)

Temperamental aircraft and pilot error occasionally created unusual accidents at Chanute Field. Maj. Tom Hanley apparently landed his LWF Model V atop a Standard SJ-1 on the ground, flipping his airplane almost over on its back and severely damaging the other. Seeing the inevitable collision, the pilot of the SJ-1 is reported to have safely evacuated his airplane before the crash. (Chanute Air Museum.)

Many aircraft accidents and incidents required repairs that could not be accomplished in the field. Thus trucks were often used to haul or tow aircraft back to Chanute Field's hangars. On September 1, 1917, JN-4 Jenny no. 1150 suffered a damaged propeller upon landing. The image above shows the broken propeller blade in the left center, with dirt visible at the tip. Upon landing, the blade hit the ground, breaking the propeller and most likely damaging the engine. Below, the aircraft's tail skid is attached to the back of a truck to facilitate towing the derelict machine back to base for repairs. (Chanute Air Museum.)

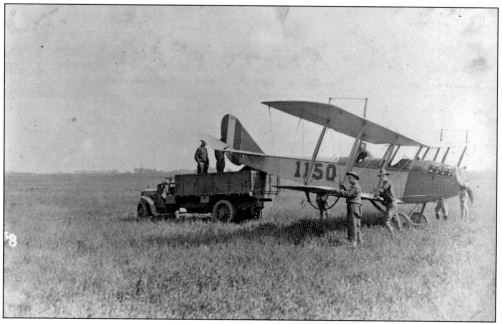

Also crashing upon landing, no. 1146 not only broke a propeller but also sheared off its landing gear. Towing was not an option, and the aircraft's wings were removed and its fuselage loaded into truck no. 35 from the U.S. Army Signal Corps, Aviation Section. The chains and mud on the truck's rear tires, wet ground showing the truck's tracks, and mud splashed on the airplane's fuselage suggest poor field conditions could have contributed to the crash. (Chanute Air Museum.)

In the early days of Chanute Field's flying mission, air-traffic control was basic and radio communication nonexistent. Shown here is the field stand for the officer in charge of flying. Guidance was relayed to aircraft in the air with large flags. A white flag signaled for a turn to the left and red flag a turn to the right. An ambulance is on standby. (Chanute Air Museum.)

On November 10, 1917, Lt. Jack M. Foote and his observer from the aircraft manufacturer H.M. Blakely flew an LWF Model V from Chanute Field to Kelly Field, Texas. They set a speed and distance record, covering 1,357 miles in nine hours and 48 minutes at an average speed of 138.4 miles per hour. The Lowe, Willard, and Fowler LWF Model V was unique compared to other trainers because of its laminated wood fuselage. (Chanute Air Museum.)

On November 1, 1917, Lt. Col. Frederick M. Jones became the commander of Chanute Field and travelled to Washington, D.C., to decide if Chanute could remain open. Upon his return, flight operations ceased on December 15, but the base did not close. This undated aerial view of a snow-covered Chanute Field hints at the poor winter flying conditions. The very fact this photograph exists, however, as well as what appear to be aircraft on the flight line show some winter flying was done. (Chanute Air Museum.)

With the suspension of flight training, many of Chanute's airplanes were transferred to other flying fields that could support year-round training. Long-distance ferry flights of aircraft were often impractical, especially when weather thwarted flying. Many aircraft were disassembled, crated, loaded onto trailers, and trucked to rail depots for shipment. Shown here engineless, and fenced in on each side by its own wings, a Curtiss Jenny fuselage rides on a highway trailer. Above, the truck, trailer, and aircraft assemblage is documented. Below, an unobstructed view is provided of the Jenny's engine radiator and empty engine compartment. The small section of "wing" above the cockpit is the airplane's fuel tank. Also of special interest are the snow chains on the truck tires. (Chanute Air Museum.)

The winter of 1917–1918 was punctuated by blizzards, 60-mile-per-hour winds, and temperatures dipping to 24 degrees below zero. Weather not only cancelled flight operations but delayed the departure of aero squadrons at Chanute destined for overseas duty in war-torn Europe. Newspapers reported these squadrons were "anxious to be doing, realizing the Kaiser cannot be whipped by them remaining in U.S. Camps." This photograph looks east toward the post flagpole. The bundled-up pedestrian and blowing flag speak to a cold wind. A sign visible in front of the flagpole reads, "Speed Limit 15 M Close Cutouts Use No Chains." (Chanute Air Museum.)

The suspension of flight training in the winter of 1917 gave birth to Chanute's most enduring strength—technical training. Morning, afternoon, and evening classes taught students the technical skills required to support a flying mission. A complete Curtiss JN-4 Jenny was assembled without the fabric skin to clearly show all of the airplanes structures and systems in place. This skeletal Jenny became a valuable training aid for aircraft mechanics. (Chanute Air Museum.)

Aircraft engine mechanics were trained at Chanute for decades. An important part of that education was the use of engine test cells to run engines away from an aircraft. Shown here is an early Chanute test cell. The engine on the stand is believed to be a Curtiss eight-cylinder, liquid-cooled OX-5. Curtis JN-4s were powered by OX-5 engines. A protective screening separates the engine from the cropped test propeller. (Chanute Air Museum.)

Automotive training was also a long-lived technical training field taught at Chanute. Shown here around 1918 is the interior of the motor transport school, or motor pool building. Men were taught the skills necessary to work on trucks, cars, and motorcycles, as well as other automotive-related skills such as tire repair and vulcanization. (Chanute Air Museum.)

Flight training resumed at Chanute on April 10, 1918. For the first time, tactical formation flying was taught, and in July night flying began. Shown here in 1918 or 1919 is a three-ship formation of JN-4s over Champaign, Illinois. The photo ship's left horizontal stabilizer is visible on the left. (Chanute Air Museum.)

Also by the summer of 1918, Chanute Field had developed an aerial photography section, teaching both the tactics and processes involved in aerial photography, which blossomed as a military intelligence–gathering tool during World War I. The aerial shot displayed above, taken in 1919, captures Chanute Field in the upper right and the village of Rantoul to the left of it. The large white building on the eastern edge of the village (center) is Rantoul's school building, and at the north end of the community (just above the airplane wing and to the right of the vertical wing strut), the Catholic Church is visible. The undated photograph below shows an unidentified farmstead north of Rantoul near the present-day Brookhill Golf Course. (Chanute Air Museum.)

As in the military today, the volunteers and recruits trained at Chanute Field in the early 1900s were young. Stanley B. Evans was likely an aerial photography trainee. Evans's portrait shows him in his "flying clothes." Above the left breast pocket of his flight suit, barely visible and believed to be written by hand in black ink, are the words "S.B. Evans Photo Section Air Base." Enlisted men, such as Evans, were as they are today—the backbone of the U.S. military. They were the workforce holding the rifles, turning the wrenches, driving the trucks, and cooking the food that allowed the military to effectively uphold the nation's defense and meet its enemies on fields of combat abroad, whether in the air or on the ground. (Chanute Air Museum.)

Life at Chanute Field was not all about flying and technical training. Soldiers from Chanute Field often ventured into Rantoul at the invitation of its citizens or visited the surrounding towns for recreation and exercise. During the summer of 1919, a group of soldiers from Chanute visited Gifford, Illinois. The image above is labeled, "Taken on a hike to Gifford, Illinois." The men have fallen out to pick blackberries on the road embankment. Below, the troops have reached Gifford and pose for a group shot out front of the R. Chumbley Grocery as they enjoy watermelon. (Chanute Air Museum.)

Taken from the roof of a hangar, this photograph of Chanute Field on parade graphically documents the magnitude of the installation's operations. Literally hundreds of men were stationed at Chanute Field, as were dozens upon dozens of airplanes. The majority of the 50 or so aircraft visible here appear to be Curtiss JN-4 and De Havilland DH-4 biplanes. (Chanute Air Museum.)

Following the end of World War I, flight training almost immediately stopped, and Chanute Field endured cycle after cycle of personnel transfers and downsizing. Chanute found itself again in jeopardy of being closed. Up until February 1921, Chanute Field reached its nadir as a dilapidated storage depot for OX-5 aircraft engines and surplus paint. Shown here, likely in 1919, is the interior of a Chanute Field OX-5 storage building. (Chanute Air Museum.)

Four

The Phoenix of Technical Training

Looking to the northwest, Rantoul and Chanute Field rest in peaceful juxtaposition on the east central Illinois prairie around 1923. Chanute's flagpole and steam plant smokestack are visible in the center. The Rantoul grade school and high school are visible just above the smokestack, and above and slightly to the left of the grade school are Rantoul's water tower and the smokestack for the light plant. (Chanute Air Museum.)

In 1867, Rantoul's school moved into a new, $6,000, two-story building on Frederick Street between Congress and Champaign Avenues. The building served both as the grade school and high school and was expanded three times. The structure was destroyed by fire in 1919. Shown here is the *c.* 1907 Rantoul High School girls' basketball team with the Rantoul school building. (Rantoul Historical Society.)

After the Rantoul school burned down, a new brick grade school was built in its place; it later became Myna Thompson Elementary. One block east on South Sheldon Street, the Rantoul Township High School was constructed. Both buildings were expanded several times and still stand today. Likely taken in 1923, this aerial photograph taken by the 5th Photo Section stationed at Chanute Field shows the elementary school in the center and the high school to the upper left center. (Chanute Air Museum.)

Taken in the 1920s, this aerial view of downtown Rantoul documents many of the area's landmarks. Along with Chanute Field, the Rantoul Township High School, grade school, and Methodist Church bell tower are visible. Sangamon Avenue bisects the frame in the center, with the First National Bank building and two-story Neal Opera House in view. The Illinois Central Railroad tracks cut across the bottom of the frame, and the Rantoul depot is in sight just below the opera house. (Chanute Air Museum.)

Along with the school system, Rantoul's downtown and business sector grew from the economic benefits of having Chanute Field as a neighbor. Looking east down Sangamon Avenue around 1927, the street has been transformed from a dirt track through a farm town to a modern, paved roadway lined with businesses, wide sidewalks, and automobiles. The First National Bank building is visible at the end of the street on the left. (Chanute Air Museum.)

In the early 1920s, the *Rantoul Weekly Press* and *Rantoul News* merged into the *Rantoul Press*. In 1927, the *Rantoul Press* merged with the Chanute Field newspaper. Shown here are the Rantoul Press Building, formerly the Rantoul News Building, and Chanute Café on Garrard Street. Chanute Field news often appeared in Rantoul's papers, and the *Rantoul Press*, having outlived the military presence, remains in operation today. (Rantoul Historical Society.)

The Illinois Central Railroad remained a staple vehicle of trade, commerce, and transportation in Rantoul, and as such the railroad depot became a village hub. Likely taken sometime during the 1920s, this photograph shows a crowd of people alongside the Rantoul depot. Since no train is present, the people are likely waiting for an incoming train. (Rantoul Historical Society.)

Even with the coming of Chanute Field and the influence of the railroad, Rantoul remained a farm town at heart, reliant on the fertile soil and the families dedicated to cultivating it. Agriculture is a way of life that defines and continues to define the character of Rantoul. Likely taken in the late 1920s, this photograph documents Allen Brines at Frank Webster's place near Rantoul weighing a load of corn. Corn is still king today, with soybeans a close second. The rectangular box houses the scale's balance mechanism and is connected to the wooden platform upon which the wagon is parked. Only the wagon is on the scale, and the horses have been pulled far enough ahead so they are standing on the ground. (Rantoul Historical Society.)

By the late 1920s and early 1930s, farm tractors began phasing out horses as the ultimate agricultural power source. This artistic photograph shows Paul Baker proudly perched atop his tractor. The machine appears to be a 10- to 20-horsepower International Harvester. The steel-tread rear wheels are caked with mud, and the power take-off wheel is just visible below the gas tank on the right. Early tractors were quite different than those seen today. Rubber tires and sophisticated hydraulic systems were in their infancy, and gasoline was the main fuel source rather than diesel fuel. Much like the development of aircraft, farm tractor evolution proceeded rapidly, culminating in the current technological marvels. (Rantoul Historical Society.)

Despite the emergence of tractors, for many farmers horses were more than simply pets or property; they were indispensable working partners on the farm, members of the family, and the literal engine of agriculture. Shown here in the late 1920s are Bess and Queen pulling a wagonload of corn driven by Ferdie Freeman. The tall side on the wagon acts as a backboard directing corn into the wagon box during loading. (Rantoul Historical Society.)

In addition to the Illinois Central and Shortline, Rantoul also had the Kankakee and Urbana Traction Company electric car line. The KUT served Urbana, Sharp's Crossing, Thomasboro, Rantoul, Ludlow, and Paxton but was never completed north to Kankakee. Operations began on December 20, 1912, and continued until March 26, 1926. The tracks ran down the center of present-day Route 45, with a depot at the corner of Sangamon Avenue. Shown here is Rantoul's KUT depot with a streetcar taking on passengers. (Rantoul Historical Society.)

In 1919, the Alfred Decker and Cohn Company of Chicago, Illinois, initiated the "world's first regular airplane express service" to deliver its Society Brand Clothes product line. On September 8, the first Rantoul stop was made when a Society Brand Clothes Curtiss JN-4D2 Jenny biplane landed at Chanute Field with a shipment for Bohlen's Clothing Shop. Shown here is that delivery. On the right is the Society Brand Clothes airplane, with ornate lettering on the fuselage and

checkerboard wings. The truck bears a placard reading, "Leonard Bros Rantoul, Ill." Wrapped packages in the truck bed suggest Leonard Brothers was picking up the delivery for Bohlen's. The car on the left is marked "USA," and the entire scene is backed by Chanute's Hangar no. 4, with a biplane visible just inside the door with "Chanute" prominently lettered on the fuselage. (Rantoul Historical Society.)

Chanute Field enjoyed a tentative revitalization in 1921. The entire Air Corps Technical School (ACTS) transferred to Chanute Field from Kelly Field. Chanute Field's mission was then forever entrenched in technical training. The mechanics, photographic, and communications schools became the three anchoring departments of the ACTS. The days of pilot training were over. The photograph above shows the airplane engine installation and repair course. Here OX-5 engines are installed in JN-4 Jenny fuselages and run up for testing. OX-5s were started by "hand propping" the propeller. The three men in a chain are pulling the propeller to start the engine. A dirt track has been worn into the ground from this type of engine starting. The photograph below shows the airplane propeller repair course. Early propellers were wooden, making mending and maintenance an exercise in carpentry. The workbench in the foreground is believed to be a jig for setting the amount of twist in a propeller blade. (Chanute Air Museum.)

Within the three main departments of ACTS, students at Chanute Field in the 1920s were not only taught the basic science of flight and proper military decorum but were also placed within one of not less than 24 different trades taught by civilian instructors. Civilians were a vital component in providing the best possible instructors throughout Chanute's long history. Shown above is parachute rigging, which required long rigger's tables and ceiling attachments. Parachute rigging and repair was one of the few fields taught at Chanute from its birth in 1917 until its closure in 1993. Below is the motorcycle overhaul course. A student's dirty coveralls warrant a comparison to the instructor's spotless suit, tie, and duster. Automotive technology and repair was another long-lived career field taught at Chanute Field. (Chanute Air Museum.)

Though the details are unclear, Chanute Field was involved with observation balloons and had a balloon hangar and mooring mast. Observation balloons were used extensively in World War I as artillery-spotting and intelligence-gathering platforms. Balloons, such as the one seen here at Chanute Field around 1923, were tethered to the ground by a winch system and capable of ascensions of 3,000 feet. Clearly visible is the occupant in the balloon's gondola. (Chanute Air Museum.)

Chanute Field witnessed and operated many prototype, experimental, and short-lived airplanes. One example of such an airplane is the Dayton-Wright B-1A biplane. On April 28, 1928, a Dayton-Wright was sent to Chanute Field for use in aerial photography training. Originally designed by Huff-Daland, the B-1A was powered by a Packard 1A-1237 engine making 350 horsepower and a top speed of 125 miles per hour. Shown here is Chanute's aircraft with its pilot. (Chanute Air Museum.)

On August 1, 1936, Martin B-10 bombers arrived at Chanute Field. The B-10 bomber was the first production bomber to enter air corps service that could outperform pursuit aircraft. It revolutionized bomber design and paved the way for the famous World War II bombers. The Martin B-10 sported all-metal monoplane construction, retractable landing gear, an internal bomb bay, full cover engine cowlings, enclosed cockpits, and rotating gun turrets. Manufactured in many variants, the main production version used at Chanute was the B-10B, which would serve into the 1940s. The photographs here show B-10s on the grass flight line at Chanute Field. In the above image, each aircraft wears nose art. Barely visible in the photograph below, on the horizon between the wing and elevator on the left, are what appear to be piles of construction materials and possibly a concrete plant, evidence of the building activity marking Chanute's renaissance. (Chanute Air Museum.)

Shown here over Chanute Field and the village of Rantoul during the mid-1930s is a Consolidated P-30 (PB-2) fighter airplane. The P-30 was the first airplane in the Army Air Corp's inventory equipped with retractable landing gear, a cockpit heater, and a turbosupercharger. Only 60 of the airplanes in nine different variants were ever built. The fore and aft two-seat cockpit configuration and the Chanute Field emblem in the white square on the aft fuselage are noticeable in this image. (Chanute Air Museum.)

POST BASKETBALL TEAM
1936-37
COACH 1ST SGT. E.J. BISHOP   ASST COACH S.SG T. W.M. GRADY

ACTS was not solely devoted to technical training, as it worked to produce well-rounded servicemen with good morale and team spirit. One mechanism used to accomplish this objective was sport. During the 1936–1937 season, on the initial cusp of Chanute Field's renaissance, ACTS fielded this basketball team. (Chanute Air Museum.)

Sports were an important pastime at Chanute Field, and that legacy would stretch through the decades. In the spring of 1918, the men at Chanute built a baseball diamond near the west boundary fence to allow the townsfolk to watch their games from the nearby road. Shown above is an early team shot of a Chanute baseball team with a De Havilland DH-4 biplane. Football was another recreational pastime at Chanute. Below, Chanute's "A" football team poses for a shot in front of the barracks no. 1 porch. In the spring of 1918, the enlisted men's barracks were expanded. The long porches became additional sleeping quarters. (Chanute Air Museum.)

A long-standing custom at Chanute Field was class photographs taken with an airplane as the backdrop. Shown here is an airplane mechanics class shot on November 13, 1936. The plane is a polished Douglas C-33, a military variant of the groundbreaking DC-2, the precursor to the famous Douglas DC-3 and C-47. Interestingly, prior to the 1940s, Chanute had no hangars large enough to hold aircraft of this size. (Chanute Air Museum.)

Another class at Chanute Field poses with the subject of it training— parachute rigging. Likely taken some time in the 1930s, the photograph shows unidentified men proudly exhibiting a parachute pack with the iconic white silk parachute and risers deployed behind them. Parachutes proved to be a vital tool, not only as an emergency system for pilots but also in safely dropping cargo from airplanes and slowing certain jet aircraft on landing. (Chanute Air Museum.)

(1)(G-6630)(5-7-37-10A)(12"-F64-3")(3-S)

The photography school was moved to Lowry Field, Colorado, in 1938 as part of the deal that saved Chanute Field in 1936. Up to that time, photography training had been a significant mission for ACTS and Chanute Field. Aerial photography was an obvious staple, but training in more conventional photographic methods and techniques was also given. Subject material for photographers in training was not always required to be military in nature; civilian subjects were also used. This shot of the Rantoul light plant and water tower was taken in 1938 by an unidentified Chanute trainee working on vertical photography techniques. (Rantoul Historical Society.)

Through the late 1920s and early 1930s, pressure had mounted to close Chanute Field. Led by W. H. Wheat and U.S. congressman D. C. Dobbins, a successful campaign was waged to save Chanute Field. But maintaining Chanute in Rantoul also meant it would need to be rebuilt. The aerial photographs shown here may be some of the last taken prior to massive cycles of rebuilding that would forever change the face of Chanute Field and lay the groundwork for Chanute Air Force Base. The image above, looking roughly northwest, was taken on November 30, 1935, and shows Chanute very much as it was constructed in 1917. The image below, looking east and taken in 1937, shows what appears to be an open house or military maneuvers. There are a large number of airplanes on the field, long lines of parked cars, and throngs of people. (Chanute Air Museum.)

Shown above is a view down one of the 1936 vintage enlisted men's barracks. Though crowded, and likely staged for the photograph, this barracks does not appear to substantiate claims of poor living conditions. The image shows white metal beds, large trunks, perforated clothes-hanging bars, and bare-bulb lighting. Without question, privacy was at a minimum and personal space at a premium. (Chanute Air Museum.)

The portal between Chanute Field and the village of Rantoul was the installation's white-arched north gate on the large curve on old Route 45. Shown here in 1933 is the northward view into the heart of Rantoul from just outside Chanute Field's north gate. Businesses locating near the area, such as the Silver Buffet and later Kings Kastles Drive-in, would benefit from the proximity to Chanute Field and the patronage of its soldiers and airmen. (Chanute Air Museum.)

This aerial photograph shows Rantoul's downtown area in the late 1930s looking west down Sangamon Avenue and across Garrard Street. The First National Bank building is prominent on the northeast corner of the intersection. On the west side of Garrard Street and to the south, the Rantoul Laundry (formerly Rantoul Press) and Chanute Café buildings are visible. The Rantoul depot and Illinois Central tracks are also visible at the top of the frame. (Chanute Air Museum.)

Especially with the economic impact of Chanute Field, Rantoul supported a vibrant and diverse downtown business district. Water's Dime Store, seen here around 1935, would endure to later become Johnson's Ace Hardware Store. Water's offered a wide range of goods from glassware and cookware to faucets and firearms to hand tools and padlocks. An ironing board and handles to children's wagons are visible at the bottom. (Rantoul Historical Society.)

A Boys Scouts of America troop was formed in the Rantoul area in 1924 and included boys whose families were stationed at Chanute Field. The American Legion was instrumental in organizing the Boy Scouts, and the legion hall was the location of early Scout meetings. Local churches also hosted meetings. This photograph shows Troop 30 of the Rantoul/Chanute Field Boy Scouts in 1932. The American flag is prominent, and the boy in the center is holding a bugle. Other interesting features of the image are the truck in the background and the boys holding white pennants with black animal silhouettes. Troop 30 is still active today, with meetings held in churches but also in Chanute's old Grissom Hall. From Tiger Scouts to Eagle Scouts, the long tradition of Scouting in Rantoul continues. (Rantoul Historical Society.)

In 1937, the U.S. Senate approved $2.8 million to begin rebuilding Chanute Field, and $50,000 in Works Progress Administration funds were allocated in 1938; appropriations quickly reached $14 million. Construction began almost immediately to rebuild Chanute into a state-of-the-art, modern technical school, which was partially fueled by available funds, partially by the grip of the Great Depression, and partially by the whispers of war drifting across the oceans. Chanute's renaissance had begun. Looking southeast in 1939, there is evidence of new construction. The large steel skeletal structures beyond the water tower are new aircraft hangars, which still stand today. The three rectangular buildings in the center are brick warehouses that are also still standing. At the bottom of the shot is Chanute's main gate, and just to the right is the shiny, rectangular Silver Buffet more commonly known as the "Bloody Bucket" made from old KUT streetcars. (Chanute Air Museum.)

Five

RENAISSANCE, WAR, AND THE U.S. AIR FORCE

During the summer of 1939, Chanute Field celebrated the U.S. Army Air Corps' birthday with a public open house. New construction is visible in the background. Also documented is the specially built railroad spur facilitating the delivery of building material directly on-site. The aircraft on the flight line are, from left to right, a Douglas C-39, North American O-47, Northrop A-17, and Martin B-10. (Chanute Air Museum.)

Also on display at the 1939 air corps birthday open house was an early model Boeing B-17 Flying Fortress, one of the first 14 ever built, and possibly Y1B-17, serial no. 37-369. The B-17 was a workhorse bomber in World War II. Chanute Field trained B-17 mechanics, radio operators, pilots, electricians, maintenance officers, and ground crews. Shown from the rear, the early B-17 gun blisters are visible. (Chanute Air Museum.)

One of the biggest challenges facing the Chanute renaissance was meeting housing requirements. Shown here in 1940 are rows of new temporary wooden barracks and support buildings still under construction. Thousands of airmen would remember their stay in these barracks and the marching required to reach their classrooms, training areas, and hangars. In later years, all of these buildings would be replaced by multi-floor brick barracks buildings. (Chanute Air Museum.)

In this aerial photograph taken in the late summer of 1940 looking south, the village of Rantoul and its tree-lined streets lie peacefully below Chanute Field. The ribbons of the Illinois Central Railroad and Highway 45 cut through Rantoul and skirt Chanute, finally splitting around the town of Thomasboro to the south in route to Urbana. Surrounding both Rantoul, Thomasboro, and Chanute Field are farmsteads in a flat sea of patchwork farm fields. Chanute is in flux—the 1917 identity and flavor still recognizable but the new and modern installation dwarfing it, crowding it out. The beginnings of paved runways and four large hangars in various stages of construction dominate the scene, as do the courtyards and walls of the massive brick barracks building nicknamed "Buckingham Palace," and to the west row after row of barracks buildings and tents and a golf course that would never be completed to make way for more barracks. What later would be recognized and known as Chanute Air Force Base had been born. (Chanute Air Museum.)

The heart of the new Chanute Field was the central grouping of buildings shown above in 1940: four large aircraft hangars, the triangular Buckingham Palace, the multi-wing hospital building with crescent shaped drive, art deco rectangular command center, and the outer ring of brick officers' houses. Perhaps the most impressive building of the group is Buckingham Palace. Built as a 2,200-man barracks, the structure was the largest building on any U.S. military installation up until the Pentagon was built. It was constructed around central courtyards with balconies and included a barbershop, café, post exchange, and mess hall. In 1967, the building was officially rechristened White Hall. The photographs here focus on the new heart of Chanute field looking northward to Rantoul, a flurry of construction still underway. (Chanute Air Museum.)

Military installations, even at Chanute prior to its resurgence, suggest coarse functionality over comfort, but not so with Buckingham Palace. Shown here in its 1940s splendor is the massive building's very own café, looking as if it could be on any street in any town in the United States. From the shiny countertop to the attendants' white shirts and ties, to the flowers and radio behind the counter, the café does not possess a stereotypical military feel. (Chanute Air Museum.)

This 1940s construction from above ground level, likely taken from the second story of an officer's house, shows mountains of building material in front of Buckingham Palace under construction. In the background are the arching roofs of the large aircraft hangars. Sidewalks and streetlights are brand new—so new that the light's globe has not yet been installed on the pole in the foreground. (Chanute Air Museum.)

A significant portion of Chanute Field's renewal construction was accomplished by the Work Projects Administration (WPA). Shown on May 31, 1941, a small army of WPA workers excavates a large storm drain box culvert at Chanute Field. No heavy equipment is in use, and the terracing and wooden bracing suggest cave-ins may be problematic. Water and mud fill the bottom of the excavation, countered by the pump in the foreground on the left. (Chanute Air Museum.)

The Headquarters and Administration Center became the nerve center of Chanute Field and would remain so throughout its U.S. Air Force days. Characterized by an art deco interior, the structure is shown here nearing completion on February 27, 1941. The post flag was prominently flown just outside the building's ornate front door, which became an important ceremonial location. (Chanute Air Museum.)

The hangar at Air School Number 3, later christened Grissom Hall, was one of the four large hangars constructed at Chanute. This hangar was an important training facility, culminating with the addition of a series of Minuteman missile training silos. Today the building houses the Chanute Air Museum, Rantoul Historical Society, Lincoln's Challenge Academy classrooms, and Rantoul Theater Group. Shown here in 1941 is the hangar's interior, complete with a compliment of Consolidated P-30s. (Chanute Air Museum.)

Even after the United States entered into World War II and driven by the war, construction at Chanute Field continued at a fevered pitch, especially to meet housing needs. Timber frame structures were built quickly and just as quickly put into use. This photograph, taken on November 17, 1942, shows the foundation of the Women's Army Auxiliary Corps (WAAC) barracks and framing for the WAAC Administration Building. (Chanute Air Museum.)

To house all of Chanute's personnel during the war, a virtual city was built on the base, dwarfing the village of Rantoul. Two-story frame barracks sprang up along with associated support buildings, but even then supplemental tent cities were still needed. Shown above is a view of the two-story barracks buildings for the special mechanics school being constructed, with a tent city visible in the background on the right and the aircraft hangars on the left. Below, temporary hospital ward buildings T-579, T-578, and T-577 are nearing completion on May 29, 1942. Of note in the images are water towers in the background, a dirt landscape, and piles of construction debris. Frame buildings such as these were remembered as poorly constructed, drafty, an inherent fire hazard, and generally uncomfortable. (Chanute Air Museum.)

Chanute's network of runways was an important component of the flying technical training mission. Paved runways replaced the grass-and-gravel landing field used previously. Later in the history of Chanute Air Force Base, the flying component of the mission would cease, and the runways were closed. Today two of Chanute's old runways are active once more, part of the Rantoul Aviation Center and Frank Elliott Field. Above, a segment of the completed runways is seen in 1942 looking to the southeast across the flight-line ramp. Below, runway construction is underway. (Chanute Air Museum.)

The technical training mission that began reinventing Chanute Field in 1921 continued to grow in scale and magnitude as the sleeping giant of the American war machine awakened to face the threats of World War II. Chanute's mission became a critical link in the chain of national defense. Taken on January 10, 1940, this image shows a master sergeant directing the efforts of his students as they change the engine in a Northrop A-17. The work is being done in one of Chanute's old wooden hangars, while the new brick hangars are still under construction. A-17s entered service in 1936 and were powered by Pratt and Whitney R-1535 radial engines. Though a good aircraft, a change in air corps philosophy in 1938 demanded twin-engine attack airplanes, so the A-17 was phased out and sold to other countries. A select few A-17 aircraft remained in U.S. service as utility aircraft and trainers until 1944. (Chanute Air Museum.)

Technological advancements continually increased the capability and effectiveness of new airplanes but also caused their systems to become more and more complicated. In this staged shot from the late 1930s or early 1940s, a class of aircraft electricians exhibits the tools of their trade, including voltmeters and a test cart for cockpit instrumentation. The aircraft is another Northrop A-17. (Chanute Air Museum.)

Training at Chanute was by necessity very hands-on in nature, but significant amounts of classroom instruction were also required. Shown here in the 1940s is a weather school classroom. The men all wear the U.S. Army Air Forces shoulder sleeve insignia, originally approved in 1942. (Chanute Air Museum.)

Under withering pressure from civil rights groups, lobbyists, newspapers, and even first lady Eleanor Roosevelt, the U.S. War Department agreed to form the first all-black pursuit squadron. Pilots were a secondary concern, because until technicians and ground crewmen were trained, a flying mission would be impossible. In March 1941, the trailblazing 99th Pursuit Squadron and Air Base Detachment 99 was constituted and activated at Chanute Field. As Tuskegee Army Air Field was not yet ready, the legendary Tuskegee Airmen were actually born at Chanute. Shown above are the first six 99th Pursuit Squadron aviation cadets at Chanute. These men would become the officer corps for the squadron. Below is a group of unidentified enlisted men from the 99th. Chanute Field was segregated, so the 99th Pursuit Squadron was relegated to old 1917 barracks, literally across the tracks from the newer, whites-only barracks. The men in both photographs are in front of Building T-39, the "Negro mess hall." (Chanute Air Museum.)

Separate training facilities and classrooms at Chanute for blacks and whites were quickly found impractical and inefficient, so instruction was integrated. Chanute was perhaps the first instance of partial integration in the U.S. military, and when the 99th transferred to Tuskegee late in 1941, Tuskegee's base commander complained that Chanute was not segregating properly. Shown above is a photograph of members of the 99th marching to or from classes down the World War I–era main street of old Chanute. Below is the 99th Pursuit Squadron's graduating class of airplane mechanics in formation outside present-day Grissom Hall. The squadron would earn the highest cumulative grade point average of any class before or since. Chanute's commander at the time, Lt. Col. Raymond E. O'Neil, said of the 99th Pursuit Squadron, "These men are good soldiers . . . this is the Army, and it is a serious business with them!" (Chanute Air Museum.)

Motion pictures have been a longtime recreational activity for the citizens of Rantoul and personnel at Chanute. The first movie theater came to Rantoul around 1916, and by the 1920s the Blackstone Theatre (in the location of the future New Home Theatre) and the Home Theatre were both showing silent pictures accompanied by piano in downtown Rantoul. The Blackstone Theatre was eventually renamed the New Home Theatre, and the original Home Theatre closed down. The first film with sound was shown in Rantoul in January 1930. The Home Theatre, shown here in 1942, became a downtown Rantoul landmark, but in 1955 it suffered a major fire. Chanute Field/AFB also had two movie theaters of its own. The Home Theatre building and marquee still stand today on Sangamon Avenue, but Rantoul no longer has an operating movie house. (Chanute Air Museum.)

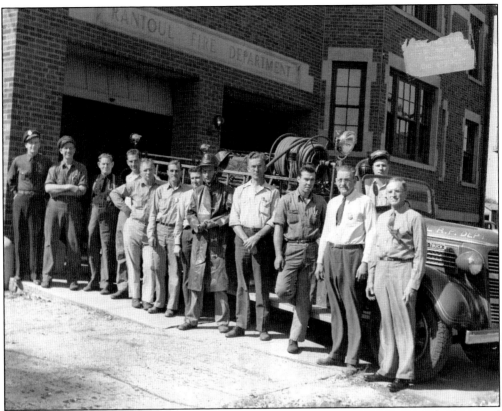

Rantoul's volunteer fire department has a long history of efficiently protecting the lives and property of the citizens of Rantoul. In addition to rescue services, the department has fought such notable fires as the 1898 and 1901 fires, the Home Theatre fire of 1955, and People's Café fire of 1957. Shown here is the 1944 Rantoul Fire Department outside the station on the lower floor of the old Rantoul Municipal Building. (Rantoul Historical Society.)

Rantoul is no stranger to severe weather. Like the blizzards that crippled Chanute Field during World War I, another struck Rantoul in 1944, burying roads, stranding cars, and creating large wind-sculpted drifts. The winds that blow across the east central Illinois prairies bring bitingly cold temperatures and blowing snow. (Rantoul Historical Society.)

For 18 weeks in the summer and fall of 1947, the merchant's committee of the Rantoul Chamber of Commerce held weekly cash drawings in downtown Rantoul. The cash prize for each drawing was $150. Shown here is one of the chamber of commerce drawings on Sangamon Avenue. In addition to the actual drawing, a band is on hand in the bed of the W. E. Terry Lumber Company truck. Chanute Air Force Base has a rich musical legacy that dates back to 1917. The country-and-western band on the truck is Chanute's very own Tony's Ramblers. Shown below is the band on stage in the back of truck. The youthful faces and smiles suggest a military no longer at war and happy to participate in the festivities of peace. (Rantoul Historical Society.)

On September 18, 1947, the U.S. Air Force was formed as the newest branch of the U.S. armed services. The U.S. Army Chanute Field was no more, and in its place Chanute Air Force Base was born. Taken on April 20, 1947, looking south, this aerial view of Chanute Field and Rantoul marks the transition between the army and air force. The central core of Chanute is anchored by Buckingham Palace, bounded on the east by runways and hangars and on the west by the massive housing area. To the north, old Chanute has faded away, as the 1917 era buildings and facilities are phased out and torn down, and eventually disappeared all together in the years to come. Rantoul has continued to grow. There is a large, new housing development on the northeastern edge of Rantoul. (Chanute Air Museum.)

Sangamon Avenue was and is the main artery into the heart of downtown Rantoul. Though the downtown business district remained within a roughly four square-block area, it became the symbol and showplace of Rantoul. Even in a world of malls and retail chain stores, Rantoul's downtown remains, albeit much quieter than in its prime. Shown here are 1950s views of downtown Rantoul on Sangamon. The above shot taken from the wide sidewalk shows a parking meter adorned with American flags to commemorate Flag Day. Outside the hardware store, push lawn mowers are on display and the Buick in the foreground wears an Idaho license plate. The photograph below, likely from the late 1950s, shows a bustling downtown, changed with time, yet still bearing the charm and feel of days gone by. (Rantoul Historical Society.)

Six

REFINEMENT IN
TIMES OF CHANGE

Another view looking east documents downtown Rantoul's vibrancy and diversity. The iconic Home Theater marquee is in the center, and there are no visible empty parking spots anywhere along the street. Longtime Rantoul residents remember that downtown merchants could supply almost any good or service. Today a trip into a larger town may be needed for shopping, but not so in the 1950s Rantoul retail environment. (Chanute Air Museum.)

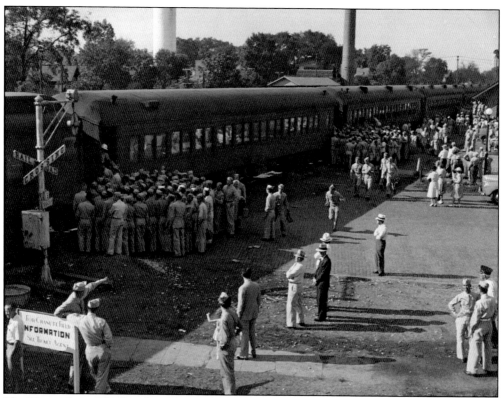

The Illinois Central Railroad and Rantoul depot remained vital for long-range military and civilian transportation. Shown here is a view of the intersection of Sangamon Avenue and the Illinois Central tracks. The Rantoul depot is visible on the right. Troops were marched from Chanute Field to the depot for embarkation. These men were likely headed to Korea or some other post supporting the war effort. (Rantoul Historical Society.)

Located at 106 North Chanute Street, the Anabel Huling Memorial Home was constructed in 1923 with money bequeathed by Madeline E. Hulling for the purpose of building a children's home in Rantoul in memory of her deceased adopted daughter, Anabel. The children's home was operated under the auspices of the Champaign County Board of Supervisors until 1976. Still standing today, the building is now home to the Anabel Huling Early Learning Center. (Rantoul Historical Society.)

In 1953 and 1954, the new wastewater treatment plant was completed east of town on Highway 136. Downtown, on Ohio Avenue north of Grove Avenue, a new water softening plant was built, and on North Maplewood Drive a new 500,000-gallon water tower was erected. Shown above is the distinctive Rantoul Water Softening Plant. Rambunctious youths found adventure in trying to run up the curved overhang surrounding the plant's front entrance. In 2006, the plant suffered a partial roof collapse, requiring major reconstruction and creating an opportunity for improvements. Below is the Maplewood water tower nearing completion in 1954. The structure was actually built twice. When nearly complete on a site near Mitchell Court, runway safety zones at Chanute AFB changed, suddenly making the tower a flying hazard. It was taken down and rebuilt on Maplewood at the government's expense. (Rantoul Historical Society.)

In 1954, Rantoul spent the year celebrating its centennial. Men grew out their beards, plays and pageants were staged, exhibitions opened, festivities held, and older folks reminisced as the proud history and progress of Rantoul was celebrated with vigor. Shown here at a centennial celebration exhibition is a young James Cheek marveling at corn plants displaying Rantoul's agricultural prowess. Some 56 years later, Cheek commented that either he had been "really short or that corn really tall." He and his family still live in Rantoul. A Vietnam veteran and longtime Illinois Central Railroad man, Cheek is currently the president of the Rantoul Historical Society. His sister Kaye retired from Chanute AFB and is the historical society's secretary and daily operations manager. The Cheek family is one of a select few with deep, long-standing Rantoul roots that have been witness to monumental historical changes. (Rantoul Historical Society.)

Prior to 1930, Rantoul's police department usually consisted of one man. Crime was low, and the duties of law enforcement were minor. However, as the town grew and more complex problems emerged, the need for an expanded police force grew. By 1954, Rantoul had nine police officers, and by 1974 that number had grown to 20. Today 34 officers serve Rantoul. Above, police chief H. O. Funkhouser (left) and a fellow officer supervise as a car is prepared for towing in 1952; the towable offense is unknown. Below is the 1957 Rantoul Police Department with other local officials. The photograph includes, from left to right, (first row) L. E. McDonald, Officer Wilson, Charles Carlton, Richard Davenport, and Eugene Morrison; (second row) Magistrate Reynolds, E. E. Drennan, Mayor Hap Parker, Chief George Hooper, Henry Peters, William Bradshaw, and Frank Pollock. (Rantoul Historical Society.)

In 1957, the Rantoul Christian Church located at the corner of Belle Street and Route 45 was torn down. Prior to demolition, the church bell was removed from the bell tower. The large crane was never unloaded from its trailer; its reach was more important than how much weight it could lift. Workmen in the tower watch as the bell is taken from the church building. (Rantoul Historical Society.)

Perhaps the most famous Rantoul restaurant was the Redwood Inn on Route 136 east of Rantoul. In its heyday in the 1960s, the establishment boasted a 50-unit motel, swimming pool, extensive gift shop, and a 600-seat restaurant. Conceived by William L. Thompson, the Rantoul Redwood Inn was one of four in the state. The eatery was famous for its homemade bread and one of the first smorgasbords in the United States. (Rantoul Historical Society.)

Skirted by Interstate 57 to the west, the main thoroughfares through the village of Rantoul are U.S. Routes 136 (Champaign Avenue) and 45 (Century Boulevard). Route 136 runs east to Gifford and west to Fisher and Heyworth. Route 45 heads south past Chanute AFB to Urbana and north to Paxton, Loda, and Buckley. This photograph shows the intersection of Route 136 and Route 45 just south of downtown around 1967. The Methodist church is the tall building in the background. Time has changed this intersection. The church remains, but today the gas stations have been replaced by a used-car dealership and a video rental store. The corner lot to the northwest, which once held the Rantoul Public Library, is now a chain drugstore. The library still exists and thrives in its new home in the elegantly remodeled former Chanute bowling alley. (Chanute Air Museum.)

Technological advances in jet propulsion during World War II ushered in the jet age, and Chanute was tasked with training jet engine mechanics. The base's first jet engine course was taught in 1946. The photograph shows students at Chanute replacing the J33 jet engine in a Lockheed P-80 Shooting Star. The P-80 was the first operational jet fighter in the U.S. Army Air Corps. (Chanute Air Museum.)

As aircraft became more complicated, training devices became important to help students understand complex systems and components outside of an operational airplane. Here training aids maintenance men work on an operational cutaway of an R-4360 radial engine for Chanute's aircraft and engine maintenance courses in the 1950s. The Pratt and Whitney R-4360 Wasp Major was one of the largest and most maintenance-intensive radial engines ever built. (Chanute Air Museum.)

9' 6" WIDTH
21' 3" LENGTH
7' 8" HEIGHT
TRAINER 6910-NL-S-AFB3018-55-01F-0-2057

The Training Devices Branch at Chanute AFB was renowned for its ability to meet the needs of the instructors. Shown here is a training aid from 1955, likely designed to demonstrate a hydraulic flight-surface control system. The aircraft tail visible on the right is that of a Republic F-84, and the large aircraft in the background is a Fairchild C-119 Flying Boxcar. (Chanute Air Museum.)

Sundry activities and career fields were required to support the technical training mission at Chanute AFB. Cooks, secretaries, security police, student work details, and countless others were required for Chanute to succeed as a multifaceted military technical training facility. Airman 1st Class Dean C. Ahrens did his part as a member of the flight-line crew refueling airplanes. He is shown here with his fuel rig in September of 1955. (Chanute Air Museum.)

In 1917, Chanute Field hosted Fourth of July festivities featuring "plenty of amusements for the young and old." In 1922, civilians were invited by Chanute to "come in the morning and stay until the chickens roost" for a daylong open house packed with facility tours, aerial expositions and demonstrations, athletic events, performances, and food. This is a shot from an open house celebrating Armed Forces Day, May 18, 1953. Looking across the ramp to the east, military

personnel and civilians are interspersed between aircraft on the flight line. The fighters being refueled at the top are North American F-86 Sabers. The F-86 served in combat during the Korean War. The larger twin-engine airplanes at the bottom are North American B-25 Mitchells. A multi-variant workhorse in World War II, B-25s remained in use at Chanute through the late 1950s. (Chanute Air Museum.)

Chanute was on the front line of the Cold War. The nuclear-armed North American AGM-28 Hound Dog air-to-ground missile, launched from under the wing of a Boeing B-52 bomber, was designed to eliminate Soviet ground defenses. An AGM-28 Hound Dog is shown here at Chanute in the 1960s with a wing pylon attached. (Chanute Air Museum.)

The Convair B-58 Hustler, first flown in the 1950s, was the first supersonic jet bomber designed specifically to deliver a nuclear weapon while outrunning ground defenses, surface-to-air missiles, and enemy fighters. Chanute AFB received its first B-58 in October 1961 and was designated as the primary installation responsible for the aircraft's combat readiness. This photograph captures the arrival of one of Chanute's B-58s on the ramp. (Chanute Air Museum.)

Fire training was transferred to Chanute AFB in the fall of 1964 after Greeneville AFB, Mississippi, closed. A burn site was soon constructed, and additional specialty courses were developed relating to operating firefighting apparatus and fighting missile-related fires. Chanute's Fire Protection Training branch evolved into one of the "world's most complete fire protection technology schools." Students were thoroughly trained to attack a building structural fire with equal alacrity as an aircraft crash fire. Shown above at the 1968 burn site, Chanute firefighters attack a simulated aircraft fire. The focus of their efforts is a burning mock-up of a B-52 bomber. The image was taken from the top of the crash truck, with the foam-covered upper turret visible in the lower left foreground. The image below records Chanute airmen firefighters debriefing after extinguishing a training fire in 1970. (Chanute Air Museum.)

In the late 1950s, F. E. Warren AFB, Wyoming, was re-tasked from a technical training center to an operational Minuteman missile site. Consequently, all of F. E. Warren's technical training responsibilities were transferred elsewhere. The vehicle maintenance and ground-powered and support equipment schools were assigned to Chanute AFB in 1958. Ground-powered and support equipment training was later renamed aerospace ground equipment training, or AGE. This photograph captures AGE students Airman Raymond Vidal, Airman Donald Crutchfield, and Airman Clifford Barker troubleshooting an M32A-10 generator cart. Many jet aircraft required an external power source for systems operation until their engines were running. Other examples of AGE equipment include air-start carts and hydraulic servicing units. (Chanute Air Museum.)

Prior to the 1970s, women were not allowed into most USAF technical training fields but were relegated to stereotypically "female" career fields such as nursing and clerical work. By 1973, however, technical training had opened up to women. Among many hardened traditionalists, the military was no place for women, but they served well and proved themselves worthy of the technical training they received at Chanute AFB. In 1979, Maj. Gen. Norma E. Brown became the first woman to command an USAF Air Training Command technical training center when she assumed command at Chanute. Shown above is a female AGE student working on what appears to be a hydraulic servicing cart, and below is one of the first women in the jet engine mechanics school. (Chanute Air Museum.)

Airman Carole Kirkland began her military career in the Royal Air Force. An officer, she was in charge of food service and catering operations. After coming to the United States, she graduated from Chanute's jet mechanics course and was an airman in the USAF Reserve. Kirkland is shown here working on a jet engine accessory in 1978. (Chanute Air Museum.)

Airman Elisa Bowls and Airman Jeffrey L. Walker, pneudraulics students, are shown here working on an F-100 Super Saber jet fighter. Pneudraulics students were taught to understand, operate, maintain, and repair aircraft systems that operated hydraulically or pneumatically. Such systems included flight-control surfaces, wheel brakes, landing-gear retraction and extension systems, and their secondary backup systems. (Chanute Air Museum.)

Even after an aircraft type was removed from the inventory, many of the original training aircraft remained at Chanute as training aides within various career fields or wound up on static display. The North American F-100 Super Saber came to Chanute AFB in 1955 to train fuel specialists and remained in various other capacities until base closure. Shown here is an F-100 being used by pneudraulic students in the 1970s. (Chanute Air Museum.)

White Hall and the main hangars remained focal points at Chanute AFB, even as other areas of the base continued to develop and grow. New brick barracks were built; a new missile building, Jackson Hall, was constructed; and Minuteman missile training silos were installed in Grissom Hall. Shown here is the modern Chanute Technical Training Center looking west across Hangar 2 and White Hall. (Chanute Air Museum.)

The kings of missile training at Chanute AFB were the Minuteman training programs, encompassing Minuteman I, Minuteman II, and Minuteman III missile systems. In the beginning, training equipment was expensive and in short supply, and qualified instructors were scarce. Chanute initially struggled to keep pace with training expectations and rapidly evolving technological advancements. Nonetheless, when the first Minuteman sites became operational in 1962, men trained at Chanute were there and from the onset were playing crucial roles in the national defense strategy of nuclear deterrence. Taken on July 28, 1970, this photograph shows a Minuteman III reentry system waiting to be lowered from a payload transportation trailer into the launch training facility at Chanute AFB. Chanute would spend millions constructing state-of-the-art missile training facilities to insure students were given the best possible training in so vital a weapons system. (Chanute Air Museum.)

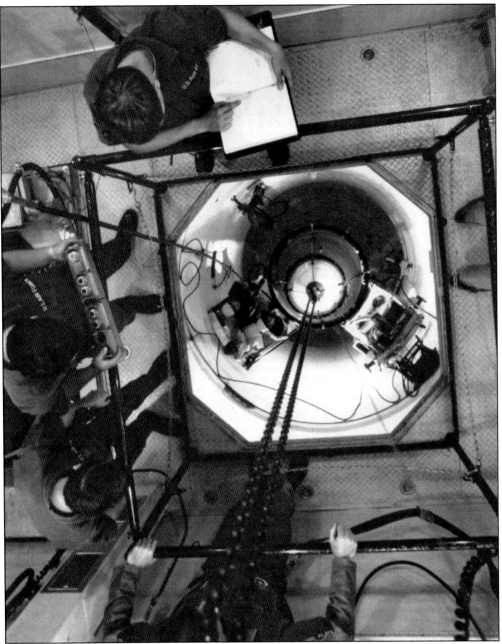

As men look on from above, a reentry system is mated to a Minuteman missile in Chanute's launch facility trainer. The Minuteman III was the first intercontinental ballistic missile (ICBM) capable of carrying multiple, independently targetable reentry vehicles (MIRV), such as the Mark 12 and Mark 12A. The reentry system was comprised of three MIRVs and chaff and flare penetration aids enclosed within an aerodynamic shroud. The MIRVS were independently aimed with a hypergolic rocket engine. Minuteman III missiles were manufactured by Boeing, their guidance systems by the Rockwell Autonetics division, and their reentry vehicles by General Electric. These weapons systems had a range in excess of 6,000 miles, with speeds topping 15,000 miles per hour and a ceiling of 700 miles. (Chanute Air Museum.)

In 1977, Chanute Air Force Base celebrated its 60th anniversary as well as its 60-year relationship with the village of Rantoul. Both base and village had grown and changed together, forging an identity and perception often inseparable from one another. Some things, however, remained constant. Chanute continued to excel at its technical training mission, and Rantoul retained its small/farm-town character. Above, Rantoul mayor Jack McJilton (left) raises a 60th-anniversary commemorative flag in honor of Chanute Field on Sangamon Avenue. Below, Rantoul's small-town character still shines through in this shot looking east down Sangamon Avenue, showing the First National Bank building and the store awnings reminiscent of downtown Rantoul from bygone days. (Chanute Air Museum.)

The link between Rantoul and Chanute Air Force Base was so strong that the winner of a contest in 1968 to design a village seal included imagery of Chanute AFB. Terrie Eberle, whose husband was stationed at Chanute, created the winning design shown here. The uniformed airman and flight of jet aircraft clearly bear witness to the importance of Chanute, but Eberle also tapped into Rantoul's other equally important identities as an agricultural community and railroad town with fields of stylized corn cut by railroad tracks heading into the horizon. By 1977, Rantoul's seal was changed to what it is today, defined by village code as "circular in form, with the words 'Village of Rantoul Illinois 1854' on the outer circle, and in the interior and center . . . a sun rising over a field with four stars radiating from the sun." (Rantoul Historical Society.)

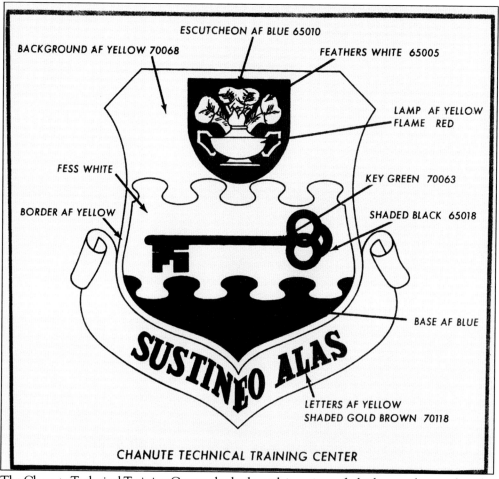

ESCUTCHEON AF BLUE 65010

BACKGROUND AF YELLOW 70068

FEATHERS WHITE 65005

LAMP AF YELLOW
FLAME RED

FESS WHITE

KEY GREEN 70063

BORDER AF YELLOW

SHADED BLACK 65018

BASE AF BLUE

SUSTINEO ALAS

LETTERS AF YELLOW
SHADED GOLD BROWN 70118

CHANUTE TECHNICAL TRAINING CENTER

The Chanute Technical Training Center also had a seal, iterations of which wound up on the sides of airplanes and as concrete decoration above building entryways. On April 7, 1966, this design was approved. The significance of the heraldry is officially described as follows: "The emblem is symbolic of the Center and its mission. The field of gold and blue signifies the excellence of Air Force operations; the nebuly fess represents the flying mission of the Air Force. The key to knowledge in the early Air Service color denotes the Center's training mission and the skill required of technicians through the years in maintaining American airpower. The honorable augmentation, the escutcheon, charged with a plume and lamp of knowledge, being the Arms of the Air Corps Technical Training School approved in 1929, commemorates the long history of technical training at Chanute." (Chanute Air Museum.)

Again during the winter of 1977–1978, Rantoul and Chanute AFB were hit by a fierce blizzard, dumping piles of wind-whipped snow and creating inconvenience and headache both in town and on base. The photographs here show Chanute's efforts to deal with the snowfall and dig-out afterwards. Heavy equipment was put to work immediately to clear roadways and thoroughfares, but for more delicate snow removal, student details armed with shovels and warm clothing were sent out. The detail shown below appears to be enjoying the change of pace while digging out a buried car. (Chanute Air Museum.)

Despite persistent rumors and previous attempts to close the facility dating back to 1917, Chanute Air Force Base appeared on a Defense Base Closure and Realignment Commission (BRAC) closure list for a second time, and in 1989 the official announcement was made that Chanute would be shut down. The technical training mission Chanute had nurtured and grown would be broken down into its component parts and disseminated to other installations. However, whether through the trials of inadequate housing, initializing Minuteman missile training, the turmoil of the Vietnam War years, or base closure, Chanute Air Force Base and its civilian and military personnel continued to provide some of the best technical training in the world, patriotically serving their country as a cornerstone of national defense as pacesetters showing the way. Shown here, a Chanute Security Police color guard addresses the colors at the base flagpole in front of the headquarters building during the 1980s. (Chanute Air Museum.)

Seven

AN END OF AN ERA BEGINS ANOTHER

The security police were responsible for all law enforcement and security at Chanute. During the late 1960s and 1970s, the base became a target for Vietnam War protestors. The security police were tasked with protecting the base and with the personal safety of military and civilian individuals alike. The photograph shown here, likely dating to the 1980s, documents a stoic security police officer and his squad car. (Chanute Air Museum.)

In 1978, army and air force fire training was consolidated at the Chanute Technical Training Center. Three years later, Chanute was designated as the Department of Defense's central fire-protection school and in 1985 was accredited by the Joint Council of National Fire Organizations. Chanute's prowess as a fire-training school led to the construction of a new fire-protection training complex, seen in this photograph. (Chanute Air Museum.)

Students at Chanute became much more than simple mechanics, they became technical specialists. Shown here in 1980 are aircraft electrical systems specialists training at Chanute. Based on the aircraft silhouette on the training board on the far right, they appear to be working with F-4 Phantom systems. On the board just above the man in the center appear to be throttle levers and a cockpit light. (Chanute Air Museum.)

Weather training was a course of study at Chanute that remained a staple through the 1980s; and not long before Chanute closed in 1993, a brand-new weather training building was completed. This photograph shows old technology meeting new. Helium- or hydrogen-filled weather balloons were a tried-and-true technology for carrying aloft expendable measuring devices (radiosondes) to collect and transmit atmospheric temperature, pressure, and humidity, but new tracking technologies and radiosonde designs greatly improved the system. Special radiosondes called rawinsondes were developed to capture wind speed and wind direction, and radar and GPS systems were developed to augment radiosonde radio tracking. The unit pictured along with the balloon is a GMD-1 rawinsonde tracker. (Chanute Air Museum.)

The Chanute Training Devices Branch also built trainers for other installations. With the development and use of the U.S. Space Transportation System, more commonly known as the space shuttle, Chanute personnel designed and built a full-scale Orbiter Crew Rescue Procedural Trainer for Edwards AFB, California. (Chanute Air Museum.)

From 1977 through 1979, the Chanute Technical Training Center became the primary training center and responsible test agency for air-launched cruise missiles (ALCM). In 1982, the first ALCMs arrived. This photograph shows a Boeing AGM-68B missile fuselage being lowered onto a stand. The AGM-68B was a nuclear-armed weapon (later converted for conventional armament) powered by a jet engine and launched from a B-52 bomber. (Chanute Air Museum.)

The Jet Engine branch continued providing vital technical training at Chanute and kept pace with rapid technological advancements and new aircraft requirements. As F-16 Fighting Falcon and F-15 Eagle jet fighters entered the inventory, powered by the modular Pratt and Whitney F100 engine, Chanute technical training accommodated them. A class in 1983 is shown working on an F100 jet engine. The F100 was capable of producing almost 30,000 foot pounds of thrust in afterburner. (Chanute Air Museum.)

In 1988, just prior to the announcement that Chanute Air Force would be closed, Airman Hope Crider, a member of the security police, provides armed security at one of Chanute's gates. Chanute had three main gates—north, west, and east—providing ingress and egress from the base. They were focal points of safety and manned professionally by the security police. (Chanute Air Museum.)

Once aircraft had served their usefulness as training aids or flyable aircraft at Chanute, many began new lives as static display aircraft located across the base. They became icons and ambassadors of U.S. Army Air Corps and U.S. Air Force heritage and touchstones for reminiscing Chanute veterans. For example, many Chanuters vividly remember marching past the colossal Convair B-36 Peacemaker on their way to and from class, and one base commander collected an example of each aircraft the Thunderbirds demonstration team had flown and had them painted in Thunderbird colors. Work details were regularly assigned to maintain these retired mechanical veterans. Cleaning and repainting became commonplace. Chanute's B-52 Stratofortress receives a wash in this photograph. Many of the Thunderbird aircraft remain at the Chanute Air Museum, while the B-36 was moved to Castle AFB, California, prior to Chanute's closure. (Chanute Air Museum.)

Following years of reorganization, the deactivation of training schools and the relocation of others, course workarounds, and waves retiring or relocating personnel, the end finally arrived. Despite gallant efforts to somehow stop the inevitable, Chanute Air Force Base closed on September 30, 1993. The U.S. Air Force was gone, and Rantoul was thrown into sadness and disbelief. The village government and an army of committees set to work on recovery. Shown here are Chanute's colors being lowered for the last time, signaling the end of a 76-year military aviation and technical training era and initiating an entirely new chapter in the history of Rantoul. Without question, the day was filled with sadness but also for Rantoul a tacit determination to survive. (Rantoul Historical Society.)

Rantoul's challenging recovery from the loss of Chanute Air Force base continues. The village successfully existed prior to Chanute and will endure and persevere in a new era after Chanute. In 1994, floodwaters submerged the Indian Hills housing development, perhaps adding insult to injury for a community still reeling from the base closure. Yet the image above suggests opportunity and promise rising from hardship, signified by the calm waters reflecting the sky—a scene easily defined as beautiful in any other setting. The Rantoul area's agricultural roots remain strong, and farmers still cultivate the rich soil and harvest bountiful crops. Though enduring several reorganizations and mergers, the Illinois Central Railroad's *I* emblem still graces an overpass in Rantoul, and freight trains continue to rumble through town pulled by locomotives like the one below. Despite Chanute's demise, some things in Rantoul remain the same. (Rantoul Historical Society.)

In 2010, Sangamon Avenue still defines downtown Rantoul, an anchor ebbing and flowing with the current of time but retaining Rantoul's character. These images look east down Sangamon Avenue, not unlike others taken before. The old First National Bank building and many of the other storefronts stoically mark time much as they did in the past and still project Lothrop's image of Rantoul as the "comely, wide-awake and inviting village" of yesteryear. (Mark D. Hanson.)

Chanute's heritage lives on at the Chanute Air Museum. Created from the turmoil of Chanute's closure and a desire to retain the former base's static display aircraft and preserve the historic legacy of Chanute AFB, the Chanute Air Museum opened to the public in 1994. Housed in old Grissom Hall, the museum's mission is simple, "The Chanute Air Museum is dedicated to collect, preserve, exhibit, and interpret aviation and aerospace artifacts. Special emphasis is directed to the life and accomplishments of Octave Chanute, Chanute Field/Chanute Air Force Base and its technical training programs, the history of Illinois military aviation, and Illinois civilian aviation." The museum holds 35 aircraft, many of which are on loan from the National Museum of the United States Air Force or the National Museum of Naval Aviation, approximately 3,000 object artifacts, over 10,200 library volumes, and an estimated 100,000 photographic images. (Mark D. Hanson)

Rantoul's history and legacy have been shepherded by the Rantoul Historical Society since 1973, for many years under the watchful eye of Geil Butler. The stated purpose of the society is to bring together people interested in history—especially the history of Rantoul, Illinois—to foster an understanding of the democratic way of life and through that understanding gain knowledge to better appreciation of American heritage. Entirely operated by volunteers, the historical society preserves and exhibits Rantoul's rich legacy with care and concern; exhibits include such subject matter as the railroad, schools, churches, fraternal organizations, businesses, and historic homes. Today the Rantoul Historical Society shares space with the Chanute Air Museum in Grissom Hall, creating an amazing partnership and collaborative cultural center rare in communities of Rantoul's size. (Mark D. Hanson.)

BIBLIOGRAPHY

Anderson, Nancy. "Chanute Grows Rapidly as War Approaches." *The Rantoul Press and Chanute Field News: Commemorative Edition*, June 14, 1976.

Butler, Geil E. *A Brief History of Rantoul, Illinois: Home of Chanute Field for 76 Years*. Rantoul, Illinois: Rantoul Historical Society, 2001.

Coates, G. Y. *A History of USAF Fire Protection Training at Chanute Air Force Base 1964–1976*. Rantoul, Illinois: Chanute AFB Technical Training Center, 1977.

Documents Relating to the Organization of the Illinois Central Railroad, 2nd edition. New York: Geo. Scott Roe Stationer and Printer, 1852.

Hansen, G. Fred. "Ordeal to Last a Decade." *The Rantoul Press and Chanute Field News: Commemorative Edition*, June 14, 1976.

Hansen, Glenn E. "Chanute Field Becomes a Reality." *The Rantoul Press and Chanute Field News: Commemorative Edition*, June 14, 1976.

Hanson, Mark D. *The 99th Pursuit Squadron: From Rantoul to Ramitelli and Beyond*. Rantoul, Illinois: Chanute Air Museum, 2006.

Illinois Central Railroad, The: A Historical Sketch of the Undertaking with Statistical Notes on the State of Illinois, the Cities of Chicago, Cairo, &c., and a Description of the Railway, Its Route and Lands. London: Smith, Elder, and Company, 1855.

Lothrop, J. S. *Champaign County Directory with History of the Same, and Each Township Therein*. Chicago: Rand, McNally and Company, 1871.

Podagrosi, Katy B. *Eye of the Storm: Chanute Closes*. Paxton, Illinois: Paxton Printing Company, 2000.

——. *Neipswah: Rantoul 1776–1976*. Rantoul, Illinois: Rantoul Press, 1975.

Rantoul Tales and Photos: 108 Personal Recollections. Rantoul, Illinois: Rantoul Historical Society, 2000.

Snyder, Thomas S. *Chanute Field: The Hum of the Motor Replaced the Song of the Reaper 1917–1921*. Rantoul, Illinois: Chanute Technical Training Center, 1975.

Starr, John W. Jr. *Lincoln and the Railroads*. New York: Dodd, Mead, & Company, 1927.

Weckhorst, Donald O. *75 Year Pictorial History of Chanute Air Force Base Rantoul, Illinois with 2006 Addendum*. Nappanee, Indiana: Evangel, 2006.

INDEX

DISCOVER THOUSANDS OF LOCAL HISTORY BOOKS
FEATURING MILLIONS OF VINTAGE IMAGES

Arcadia Publishing, the leading local history publisher in the United States, is committed to making history accessible and meaningful through publishing books that celebrate and preserve the heritage of America's people and places.

Find more books like this at
www.arcadiapublishing.com

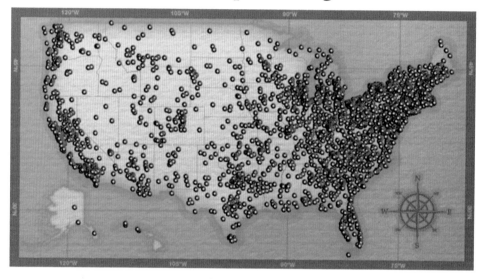

Search for your hometown history, your old stomping grounds, and even your favorite sports team.

Consistent with our mission to preserve history on a local level, this book was printed in South Carolina on American-made paper and manufactured entirely in the United States. Products carrying the accredited Forest Stewardship Council (FSC) label are printed on 100 percent FSC-certified paper.

MADE IN THE